THE BLUE STORE

THE BLUE STORE

By

Country Ranch Writer

Copyright 2018, Country Ranch Writer

All rights reserved. Printed in the U.S.A.

No part of this publication may be reproduced or transmitted in any form or by any means, electronic or mechanical, including photocopy, recording or any information storage and retrieval system now known or to be invented, without permission in writing from the publisher, except by a reviewer who wishes to quote brief passages in connection with a review written for inclusion in a magazine, newspaper or broadcast.

Published in the United States
by eBooks2go, Inc.
1827 Walden Office Square, Suite 260, Schaumburg, IL 60173

ISBN-10: 1-5457-4251-0
ISBN-13: 978-1-5457-4251-8

Library of Congress Cataloging in Publication

CONTENTS

Prologue vii

Chapter 1: Moonshine and Bluegrass 1
Chapter 2: Timeless Memories 5
Chapter 3: Jake Gets Nosey 9
Chapter 4: Jake Hikes Up the Mountain 13
Chapter 5: Jake Returns Home 17

PROLOGUE

Times were hard for the folks up in the hill country and this story is about moonshining during the life and times of the folks there. Grandma Ivy runs the only store for miles around. You will read about family and friends gathering there to find hope, joy and understanding and a bit of country music thrown in.

CHAPTER 1

MOONSHINE AND BLUEGRASS

ON ANY GIVEN WEEKEND you could find the folks from the mountains all around gathered here to play their music. The Blue store here was deep down in the hollow along the creek. Roads weren't much in the way of being passible at times. Especially during the rainy season. It had a reputation for being the local hangout for all those who liked Bluegrass Music and Shine.

You came dressed as you are and no fancy cover charge to ever worry about like in the big cities. It was place for one and all, families and children included.

The area around here is rugged and remote so everyone here traveled mostly by foot. Those lucky enough to own a car or pickup trucks were considered fortunate. Many of the cars found here were shine hauling cars and the fastest on the mountains. They were equipped not only to go fast but to haul the biggest loads of shine available. They used their cars in races to find out who had the faster car in the mountains. On weekends you could see the shiners racing for pink slips and arguing who had the best cars.

Later down the road, it would be the beginning of the race car era with many moonshiners like Junior Johnson and others

Chapter 1

involved. Their racing started with them arguing over who was the better runner with the fastest car. Junior Johnson has played a big part in the moonshine business. Junior was overheard one day saying to another bootlegger; I was only 12 when I was hauling booze." The other bootlegger Cal said," was a hauler and said, "back then we didn't need a drivers license. If we got caught we'd just hop out and run." Johnson says with much pride to his friend; that he never lost 'A race," to the law.

Many banjo pickers and players have been known to sing and play for their supper a time or two while traveling through down at the Blue Store.

Bluegrass music and moonshiners went hand and hand back in the day making a living doing what they do best.

While the music was playing the shine was selling out the backhand over fist. Surprisingly no one ever got caught. The Blue Store held dances and bbq's every weekend and a good time was had by all. I guess that is why they say they are picking and grinning like on Hee Haw!

I remember my Grandpa used to like to play his banjo when he'd bring us down to the Blue Store. My Great Grandpa Benjamin never cottoned to it and said, "it was nothing but tomfoolery!" But, yet again, if you looked down at his foot it would be tapping away to the music. This is one thing Great Grandpa Benjamin didn't get around to teaching Grandpa.

Grandpa could play mandolin, guitar, and banjo, his most favorite instrument was the mandolin. Great Grandma Gwendolyn loved to hear Grandpa play and he always made sure he played her favorite songs. Grandma was partial to the guitar and she and Grandpa would sing while she did her knitting. She said it soothed her nerves and took away the worries of the day.

The Blue Store I learned last time I visited had been sold over the years and the new owner said, "He found it a delightful undertaking. The property had a history which he intended to preserve and there was ample room for expansion. He said he wanted to recreate the feeling the place had many year ago."

Progress still has not caught up with the area and remains untouched to the naked eye but we all know it has changed by the way people have moved on with their lives and the deaths that have taken place over the years gone by. Most of the older folks have passed on leaving their legacy to their kinfolks to carry on.

With the passing of time moonshining has now become old school and outdated. With the help of the old moonshiners shutting down their operations and going legal it has come a long way in keeping folks out of the jails.

Back in the day moonshine was made to keep the family fed due to lack of income in the farming community. They had all that extra corn to deal with so why not make something profitable to sell. For them, it was the making of moonshine.

Moonshine for them was really easy to make they just had to figure out how to out-smart the Feds and they became very good at it. You see the sugar and corn sales were suddenly monitored by the Feds to see who was using more than they were allowed by the government. It was the era of the depression so everyone was on rations back then. They came up with bartering amongst themselves for what they needed in exchange for the sugar and corn.

Coming back to visit was on my bucket list I just hadn't been back because life got in the way in one way or another. Now there will only be the memories of growing up and all the escapades my family has managed to mull through over the years. Great Grandpa Benjamin was known to be a very rough man cut from a different cloth from my Grandpa. My Grandpa was a sweet caring man and was a dear to me. He never stood in judgment and stood by me when I chose to ride horses over moonshining! Yes, hard as it is to believe girls do make and sell moonshine and used to run their own stills just like the men. That is for another time with the folks.

Some of these quaint small towns began as post-revolutionary war settlements. The Blue Ridge Mountains is dotted with small towns and cities that have been officially designated a Historic site.

Chapter 2

TIMELESS MEMORIES

Growing up around the Blue Store everyone from near and far remembered Grandma Ivy. This was the only name she was ever known by all that knew her. "Welcome to the Blue Store!" she would call out to all who entered. She was a petite lady with fire red long wavy hair with a temper to match if riled. She was five foot if she was a day and eyes like a hawk. No one dared put anything over on her. It was amazing she put people at ease right away. She made everyone feel at home and treated them all special.

None one could deny she was a beautiful woman the years had treated her kindly; yet if you looked deeply into her eyes they looked sad. She'd been through so much in her lifetime. She never talked about her life to anyone. She was the one who did all the listening to folks there at the Blue Store. People loved the food there. There wouldn't be a crumb left on their plates when they finished eating. It always made her swell with pride when they complimented her on her cooking.

I was back here in the mountains to pay my respects and visit when I ran into this guy at the Blue Store.

"You new around here?" he asked.

Chapter 2

"No, I replied, "Growing up around here was the best twenty years of my life," I said simply.

The reporter looked at me in wonder. He was here on the mountain to do a story of the old days and moonshining. "Tell me more," he probed.

I finished half of my cup of coffee and then got up excusing my self. All the reporter wanted to do was talk digging for dirt about folks. The reported slipped his recorder back in his pocket and exited the cafe disappointed.

It had begun to rain cats and dogs as I reached my truck; so much for a beautiful day the weatherman promised.

The reporter phoned his boss, he was not pleased with him at all. Can you give me a reason why I should keep paying you?" Then he said, "Well, do your best and keep me posted."

He held on to the phone for a moment after the boss disconnected. This is one story he desperately needed.

Arriving home I put my laptop on the coffee table and began a background search on the reporter and his credentials. I clicked on and his picture appeared. I scanned the bio below it, heaving a sigh of relief. He was exactly who he said he was. "Well thinking to myself, it makes me feel a bit better." Picking up my coffee mug I poured myself another cup of coffee.

The reporter parked his pickup near the door of his hotel room and climbed out. Rain lashed at his neck and tossed his hair away from his face. Hiking the collar of his denim jacket against the wind, he dashed to his room. "So here you are," he muttered grabbed his bottle of scotch and took a good swig. He took a long pull from the bottle and grimaced. Here it wasn't even noon and he was drinking.

"Well, what did you expect? Going up into the hill country; did you expect them to welcome you with open arms?" He laughed to himself.

The next morning the reporter showed up at my table hat in hand. "Can you help me?"

"I don't know," I said.

What is it you are after mister?

"The name is Jake Hollister ma'am," I am a reporter for the Country Crier. I am doing a feature on the back hill country store. "The Blue Store to be exact," Jake informed her.

So, what would it hurt to find out what he had to say?

"Why," I asked him.

Because I was told this is where the moonshiners liked to hang out. My boss wants the lowdown on what went on here in the mountains. It is a pet peeve of his. He is a fan of theirs and wants to know everything about them and their lives and what made them moonshiners. So, why did his conscience twinge? And why did he feel he was using her?

I told him let's get one thing straight If I agree to help you it will be on my terms.

For the first time since Jake met her, he felt a ray of hope. I have to go to a meeting he told me and said, "I will meet you back here at eight."

"Okay, I will meet you here later." saying goodbye to him he left.

Later as they sat at the table in the cafe he said, "I think we'd better get started. You ready?

"As ready as I'll ever be." She sat drinking her coffee...

"Okay, let's start with telling me what you know about the folks who lived here and what it was like growing up here." Jake began his interview.

There were so many people in my life growing up so it will be hard for me to single out just one. You must understand shinning was a way of life for most folks. Times were hard on everyone here in the mountains. At the age of fourteen, I could outrun any officer I met out on the back roads.

"Wait a minute," Jake said, "You are telling me you were you of all people were a shinner?"

"Well, you wanted to know," I replied. The agent's cars were no match for our cars. "My Great Grandpa Benjamin was a moonshiner and my Grandpa was in it too. When I became of age I quit moonshining and went to barrel racing.

"Why were you all called moonshiners to begin with?" Jake wanted to know.

Moonshine was made during the moonlight hours. Slang name for moonshiners was rotgut, firewater, panther piss, mountain dew, white mule, corn likker, white lightning, hooch, white whiskey, I am sure there are others.

"WOW!" Jake said, I never knew that tell me more.

CHAPTER 3

JAKE GETS NOSEY

WELL, I SAID to Jake it's getting late we'll take this up another day about the Blue Store. Right now I must be on my way. Bidding Jake goodbye I left him sitting there in his chair at the cafe. He was going over his notes. The rain had quit and so the rain had cooled off a bit.

Going home I didn't pay attention to much attention putting my truck through its paces. The drive home only took twenty minutes, but I didn't remember any of it. I was thinking of the events of the day. Jake was easy to talk to and I really enjoyed his company. He was different from other reporters that's for sure. He wasn't the stuffy kind he was more relaxed. Jake finished his notes then ordered supper for himself. He hated to cook and he wanted to try the cooking at the cafe. He was so surprised it was so delicious!

He started to smile as he thought of her. He hadn't been able to get her out of his mind. Jake put his notes in his briefcase and headed for home after he paid for his supper leaving a generous tip for the waitress. Jake looked to the heavens as he heard the roll of thunder over the hills. The wind played havoc with his hair tossing it back over his face. He made a mental note to get his hair

Chapter 3

cut. Once again he looked up at the heavens as the rain started to fall thick drops splattered on the ground. He made a beeline for his truck just making it in time. Jake couldn't wait for tomorrow to get here soon enough so he could see her again.

Later looking in the mirror I stared at my reflection. Small creases lined my brow, noticing my green eyes sparkled. Thoughts of Jake ran through my mind, smiling as I brushed the tangles from my hair. My feelings for Jake were making me feel uneasy. I hardly knew him yet I felt I had known him all of my life.

Later the next day Jake said, "Now tell me about your life."

"What about it?" I said. You mean in my spare time? Between riding and training my horses, I have no free time. Besides, I thought we were here to discuss people who live around the Blue Store. Jake said well, "you are part of the Blue Store too." So let's talk about the folks in your life.

There are Grandpa Benjamin and Grandma Gwen they are the oldest living relatives. Great Grandpa was not the easiest to live with. He was very gruff and very hard to get to know. He was very active in the moonshining business till he almost got caught by the law. He was right up there with Junior Johnson and POP Sutton. Junior was what they call a tripper, he worked for his daddy hauling shine up and down the mountains. When he wasn't running shine he could be found racing for Nascar.

I pointed to Jake to take a look around the Blue Store; it was a perfect sanctuary for moonshiners because of its rugged landscape, deep hollers, caves, creating the best places to hide the moonshine stills and everything from the law. Grandpa was a shinner following in his father's footsteps and his fathers before him. Grandpa was way different from his father for he was soft-hearted and he sure loved Grandma so. He always wore his flannel hat kind of like the one Jed Clampett used to wear his bib overhauls no matter what business he was conducting along with his old flannel shirt. He played music with his friends up at the Blue Store on the weekends. Grandma loved his playing and always attended without fail.

I told Jake it was nothing for folks to hear sounds of cars thundering down the roads going past the Blue Store. Some say movie folks came from miles away to make their films upon the mountains. Moonshiners like Tickle, Mark, and Digger were filmed by the folks. They lived by their own rules, they were free spirits and enjoyed being free.

I explained to Jake in the hills moonshiners was more than just making money it was a tradition. It was handed down from generation to generation to the other. Sutton said, "a moonshiners life is a hell of a life for some when you have nothing to lose. Some say it's a hell of a life if you have children and a wife." Jake said, 'can you think of anyone one else?' Well, there was Jo Jo, she could feel his eyes on her as she drank her coffee.

"What about him?" Jake asked.

He always tried to outdo me, he always had a way of rubbing me the wrong way. He was such a show-off and hated it when he didn't win. Jake thought it best to change the subject. He said let's take a walk up the mountain tomorrow and see if we can find some of the old stills. I would like to see if there are any remnants still around. Okay, I said let's make it a date. I said. I will meet you back here in the morning and have breakfast and then we will go exploring.

Chapter 4

JAKE HIKES UP THE MOUNTAIN

Jake said. "I would like to go see if we can find any remains of the old still from years ago."

"Okay," I said, Back in their time the stills were worth a king's ransom, just don't go selling them short. Although some moonshiners had to keep on the move they really loved their work.

Jake asked. "Is it true America's tastemakers the moonshiners, are fiercely loyal to the traditions and history of those came before them?"

"Yes," I said proudly.

They are having a Jamboree up at the "BLUE STORE" this weekend I told him. "I think you will be interested in. You can take all the notes you please," I teased him.

Jake felt his mouth edging into a smile. It was the last thing he expected was an invite from her.

He went to town and bought some new clothes for the occasion, hoping to fit in. Instead of suits, he switched to a pair of tan wrangler jeans, a short sleeve western shirt he even sprung for a pair of western boots.

Chapter 4

I had to admit he looked quite fetching when I saw him all dressed for the occasion; smiling he was all ready to go.

As we headed out to the jamboree I told Jake the folks were dedicated to keeping the moonshining spirit alive. The moonshine mountain festival is one the Appalachians regard the most authentic music celebration.

I think you will like the stories they tell of the history of moonshine being made back in the old days in the foothills. I told him that the moonshiners he will meet are the real deal and not to be surprised when he sees some familiar faces.

He said, "familiar faces?"

"Yes, those of Pop Sutton, Tickle, and Digger," I told him they had done a TV special awhile back on moonshining. He hadn't known anything about it, which I thought seemed odd. Of course, my Grandpa would be showing up to. He would be right in the mixed of things playing his music. I told him my Grandma would be riding in with us.

He just shrugged and said, "whatever."

Jake, was hoping to get to spend this time gathering more information for his research and getting to know her a little better.

The next day as planned Jake met her up at the BLUE STORE it promised to be a sun fun-filled day for their outing into the backcountry. I started walking upstream and hadn't gone very far when I spied an old still buried far down in the creek bed. Pointing to the stream she showed Jake her find. Pulling out his recorder from his pocket, he began to describe in detail their findings. Jake was so amazed he was in awe walking and talking as they continued up the creek. I pushed through the thickets as the terrain got steeper. I finally came to a bend in the creek another surprise waited for us there at the bottom was another moonshine still lying there rusting in the creek. I stopped and changed direction on purpose and Jake never had a clue why. We were getting close to my old stomping grounds. Just up the creek aways happened to be where the hidden waterfall was. It was where Great Grandpas still blew up. I shuddered too think what could've happened that day.

On the way back down the mountain, Jake turned off his recorder, stopped suddenly, looking all around him. He took in a deep breath then, exclaimed how beautiful his surroundings were. Suddenly he was pointing out to the woodpecker working away on the far tree. When he came face to face with a wild deer who walked right out in front of him! He was so close he could have reached out and pet him on the nose.

"He whispered to me," He's beautiful. He then the deer took off for parts unknown. Wow! is all he could say. It was getting late, so I reminded Jake we better get back down the mountain before it got dark. We didn't want to be stumbling around up there with no flashlight. Pulling out his recorder he told me okay and began talking to the recorder about his experience. He had a big smile on his face and looked so handsome. Shaking my head, I reminded myself he was here for a story and nothing else.

Getting back to the **BLUE STORE** we entered the cafe portion of the store and had a late supper of fried chicken, mashed potatoes, gravy, corn on the cob, hot biscuits with honey and coffee. For dessert, we had Grandma Ivy's famous apple pie.

Agreeing to meet back once again at the **BLUE STORE** we both called it a night Jake walked me to my truck before he headed for his it was turning off chilly. It would soon be winter time here in the mountains.

The leaves had already turned now falling to the ground everywhere you looked.

Chapter 5

Jake Returns Home

Reaching home, I put the kettle on for tea. Turning on the news I was shocked. Just five miles down the road from my dad police had arrested some folks for making moonshine. The newscaster said it was straight out something that would have happened in the old days. He was shocked it was still going on in this day and age. The deputies had raided a moonshine still destroying the still. He went on to say over 2,000 gallons of white liquid was seized.

The newscaster went on to say that in today's news that the moonshiners said they thought that shinning was considered a hobby. The three people were selling it at their roadside market in the remote parts of the county.

I then thought of Jake he would have a field day with this information. I wondered if he heard it on the news. I picked up the phone and called my dad and asked him what was going on. He said Jo Jo and a few others were the ones who were caught. He said they didn't even try to hide it or anything. Dad went on to say they seemed proud of the whole thing. They even went as far as to show them his still.

"What!" I said in disbelief are they crazy!

Chapter 5

"Yup, it's true," he said. Jo Jo told them how it was handed down from generation to generation and he inherited it from his dad/ He then went on to tell them it was just a hobby for him really. They were still in jail for lack of funds to get them out.

All I could say was, my goodness he knew better! I almost laughed out loud over his stupidity. He wouldn't be trying to outshine folks from now on.

Jake turned on the TV when he got back to the hotel. Making himself a drink he spit and spewed his drink out when he heard the news of the bust. What the hell did he just hear? As he sat down, he turned up the news and listened in disbelief. Were people up here in the mountains that stupid. He couldn't wait to talk to me the next day he picked up the phone and called me. He said, "Did you hear the news?" He was all excited. I told him to slow down and take a deep breath! He rushed on asking if I knew him. I reminded I talked of him in passing when he was writing his notes one day. I could hear him flipping his pages as I spoke. He said you did, didn't you? "Do you think he'd let me interview him and his friends?"

The next day Jake was all fired up. He asked what moonshine tasted like.

"Well", I said, "You might say it is history in a mason jar."

He asked, "Do you think it possible I could get some to taste?"

I just looked at him and said really?

He said, "It is for research." I am writing about moonshine he says sheepishly; I may as well know what it tastes like and what it is I am writing about.

"Okay," I know a guy who knows a guy. I told him it wouldn't come cheap, it would cost him at least $25 bucks and the good sense not to ask where she got it from and not to ask any questions or the deal was off. Laughing I said, "it is hard to believe I used to boost bootleg whiskey when I was a kid." I used to haul shine in my car down the mountain when I was fourteen. I left for a while and came back with some whiskey what he didn't know wouldn't hurt him. I got the liquor from my dad. He started to ask where I been and threw up my hand not to ask. Well, talk later, for now just take a small sip. Don't gulp it you'll be spitting and sputtering half the night. Just let a little bit slide between your lips. This is a peach flavored whiskey. You might even taste the fruit, but right behind it comes the fire. I said, that taste right there helped build our state. It helped define our history. Today in some places it still thrives you just got to know where to find it.

Jake put the lid back on the jar blushing, he said, "Wow, it packs a wallop he said. "Moonshine is not sweet tea!"

I laughed at him grinning I agreed it sure wasn't to be trifled with. Shine has to be done in moderation.

Jake was beginning to feel there is more to THE BLUE STORE than meets the eye. I told him if the BLUE STORE could talk it would give him more information than I ever could.

Making moonshine has never been an easy life told him back in my day when I was doing it you could make a gallon of whiskey for a dollar and sell it for three or four dollars. I later took Jake down to the jail if he was lucky and played his cards right these characters will give Jake an interview about how they got started in shinning and about their life as a shinner.

Jake discovered people will tell you their secrets about moonshine, as long as they knew you were no threat to them. They are proud of what they make.

It was Saturday Jake was chomping at the bit to get to the Country Jamboree. He was like a kid at a candy the store he wanted to see and taste everything. There was a lot of music, races, and he noticed at times somebody would pull out a mason jar and pass it around. Jake realized just how much moonshine was a part of their culture.

Jake had to admit he thought it was mostly legends over exaggerated hype that was until he was in the midst of it himself. It sure made a believer out of him. This was the best assignment, he ever had. These characters were the real deal and he hoped he could do justice writing about THE BLUE STORE and the people who frequented it.

After leaving the mountain Jake had a meeting with his boss who praised him for doing such a good job on his story. Jake pulled a jar out of his briefcase and told his boss as he handed the jar over to him. There is a lot of history in that jar. Go ahead, Jake told him to take a sip. It is for sipping he told his boss.

www.ingramcontent.com/pod-product-compliance
Lightning Source LLC
Chambersburg PA
CBHW030534080526
44586CB00011B/436